1,000,000 Books

are available to read at

Forgotten Books

www.ForgottenBooks.com

Read online
Download PDF
Purchase in print

ISBN 978-0-331-04886-5
PIBN 11102445

This book is a reproduction of an important historical work. Forgotten Books uses state-of-the-art technology to digitally reconstruct the work, preserving the original format whilst repairing imperfections present in the aged copy. In rare cases, an imperfection in the original, such as a blemish or missing page, may be replicated in our edition. We do, however, repair the vast majority of imperfections successfully; any imperfections that remain are intentionally left to preserve the state of such historical works.

Forgotten Books is a registered trademark of FB &c Ltd.
Copyright © 2018 FB &c Ltd.
FB &c Ltd, Dalton House, 60 Windsor Avenue, London, SW19 2RR.
Company number 08720141. Registered in England and Wales.

For support please visit www.forgottenbooks.com

1 MONTH OF FREE READING

at

www.ForgottenBooks.com

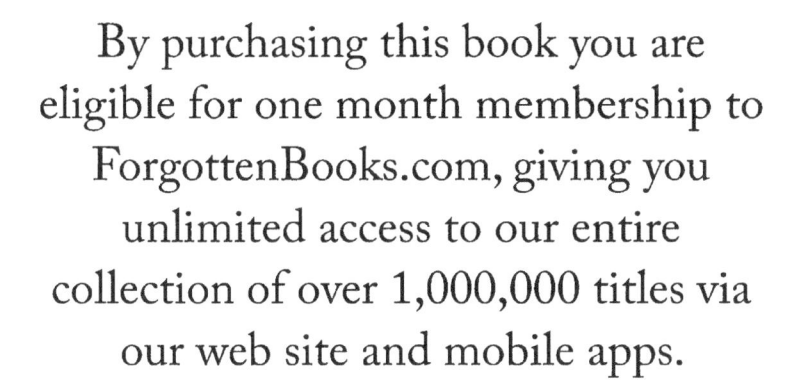

By purchasing this book you are eligible for one month membership to ForgottenBooks.com, giving you unlimited access to our entire collection of over 1,000,000 titles via our web site and mobile apps.

To claim your free month visit:

www.forgottenbooks.com/free1102445

* Offer is valid for 45 days from date of purchase. Terms and conditions apply.

English
Français
Deutsche
Italiano
Español
Português

www.forgottenbooks.com

Mythology Photography **Fiction**
Fishing Christianity **Art** Cooking
Essays Buddhism Freemasonry
Medicine **Biology** Music **Ancient Egypt** Evolution Carpentry Physics
Dance Geology **Mathematics** Fitness
Shakespeare **Folklore** Yoga Marketing
Confidence Immortality Biographies
Poetry **Psychology** Witchcraft
Electronics Chemistry History **Law**
Accounting **Philosophy** Anthropology
Alchemy Drama Quantum Mechanics
Atheism Sexual Health **Ancient History**
Entrepreneurship Languages Sport
Paleontology Needlework Islam
Metaphysics Investment Archaeology
Parenting Statistics Criminology
Motivational

Historic, archived document

Do not assume content reflects current scientific knowledge, policies, or practices.

Marketing Costs and Margins for
CHICKEN FRYERS AND FOWL

Sold in Chicago and
Minneapolis -- St. Paul

Marketing Research Report No. 195

UNITED STATES DEPARTMENT OF AGRICULTURE
Agricultural Marketing Service
Marketing Research Division, Washington, D. C.

Preface

This report on marketing costs and margins for chicken fryers and fowl is one of several reports on food items that have been, or are planned to be, published by the U. S. Department of Agriculture. These reports are designed to meet, in part, a need for information on farm-to-retail price spreads on food.

Congressional committees, labor groups, farmers, consumers, and others have turned to the Department for explanations of changes in prices and price spreads and for explanations of the components of margins. This report presents findings of research on marketing margins for chicken fryers and fowl in two large metropolitan areas. Problems closely related to margins and costs, particularly trade practices, are also treated.

The author is grateful for the assistance of Leo R. Gray and Owen F. Beeder, of the Agricultural Marketing Service, in the fieldwork of this study, and for the cooperation and assistance of the many processors, wholesalers, and retailers of chicken fryers and fowl who supplied most of the information on which this report is based.

Issued November 1957

Contents

	Page		Page
Summary	iii	Marketing practices—Con.	
Why and how the study was made	1	Refrigeration	11
		Deliveries to stores	11
Costs and margins	2	Related information	11
Fresh fryers, ready to cook	2	Handlers of live poultry	11
		Location of concentrated broiler-producing areas	12
Frozen fryers	5		
Fresh fowl	8	Distribution of broilers to consuming areas	12
Frozen fowl	9		
Marketing practices	9	Per capita consumption	13
Advertising	10	Location of processing plants	13
Determination of purchase price and selling price	10		
Surplus stocks	10	Appendix	14
Markings on displays	11	List of tables	14

For sale by the Superintendent of Documents, U. S. Government Printing Office
Washington 25, D. O. - Price 15 cents

Summary

This study describes the 1955–56 margins and operating costs of processors of chicken fryers and fowl shipping into the Chicago, Ill., and Minneapolis-St. Paul, Minn., metropolitan areas, the margins and costs of poultry wholesalers, and the margins of chain and independent retailers in those areas.

The farm-to-retail price spread for icepacked fryers moving through processors, wholesalers, and independent retail stores was 20 to 22 cents a pound. When large volumes of fryers moved directly from processors through chain retailers, the spread was 15 to 16 cents a pound in Chicago and 19 to 20 cents in Minneapolis-St. Paul. For fryers sold through both types of stores, farmers in Georgia, Alabama, and Arkansas received an average of 30 cents per pound (ready-to-cook weight). Farmers near Chicago received 33.3 cents per pound, and those in the Minneapolis-St. Paul area received 32.3 cents per pound.

Frozen eviscerated fryers moved through southeastern processors, wholesalers in or near Chicago and Minneapolis-St. Paul, and independent retailers with an overall marketing margin of 36 cents. The spread when this commodity moved from southeastern processors directly through chains was 27½ cents a pound in Chicago, and 33 cents in Minneapolis-St. Paul. When this commodity moved through frozen food processors and chainstores, the spread was about 5 cents a pound higher.

This study indicates that most handlers, processors, wholesalers, and retailers operate on relatively narrow margins for fresh, icepacked poultry.

Processors of icepacked fryers in Alabama, Arkansas, and Georgia operated on an average margin of 7.7 cents a pound. An additional half cent should be added for transportation to Minneapolis-St. Paul. Their operating costs averaged 6.75 cents a pound, leaving a net operating return of 0.95 cent a pound for the 4 months, which represented profit before taxes and a reserve for less profitable periods.

Processors within a 200-mile radius of the two consuming areas had an average operating margin of 8.0 cents a pound and total operating costs of 7.8 cents a pound. Labor costs were 1 cent a pound higher in these areas than in the southeastern areas. Labor in the receiving, dressing, and packaging operations represented 38½ percent of the total operating costs.

Wholesalers of chicken fryers in Chicago and Minneapolis-St. Paul operated on an average margin of 2½ cents a pound eviscerated weight. Salaries and wages represented 64 percent of their operating costs. As most of the operations they perform are handling operations, salaries and wages represent a high proportion of their total costs.

Independent retailers of fresh fryers, ready to cook, in Chicago had an average margin of 10.9 cents a pound, and in Minneapolis-St. Paul, 10.3 cents a pound. Chain retailers in Chicago had an average margin of 8.5 cents a pound, compared with 11.0 cents in Minneapolis-St. Paul. Intense competition in Chicago held retail chain margins low.

Alabama, Arkansas, and Georgia processors of frozen broilers operated on an average margin of 17½ cents a pound, of which approximately 17¼ cents was operating costs (see tabulation page 7). Labor for receiving, dressing, and packaging was nearly a fourth of the total cost. Packaging, labor for receiving and dressing, plant overhead, delivery, and advertising accounted for about 75 percent of the operating costs.

Frozen food distributor-processors had about the same plant operating costs as southeastern distributors. But their distribution costs were higher.

Wholesalers of frozen poultry operated on margins of 6 percent in Chicago and 4 percent in Minneapolis-St. Paul. Independent retailers had margins on frozen poultry of 13 percent in Chicago and 14 percent in Minneapolis-St. Paul. Margins of chain retailers were 10½ percent in Chicago and 15½ percent in Minneapolis-St. Paul.

Processors of fresh eviscerated fowl in and near these two urban areas had an average margin of 7.0 cents in Chicago and 8.5 cents in Minneapolis-St. Paul. Operating costs on fresh eviscerated fowl and fresh eviscerated fryers were about the same. Wholesalers of fresh eviscerated fowl had an average margin of 3.7 cents a pound in both metropolitan areas.

Processors of New York dressed poultry in Minneapolis-St. Paul had an average margin of 9.5 cents a pound. Their net operating return was 1.5 cents a pound, the most profitable figure for processors covered by the study.

Independent retailers of fresh eviscerated fowl had average margins of 9.7 cents and 9.0 cents a pound in Chicago and Minneapolis-St. Paul, respectively. Chain retailers operated on a margin of 10.3 cents in Chicago and 14.3 cents in Minneapolis-St. Paul. Competition between chains and large supermarkets held the margin in Chicago about 4 cents a pound below the margin in Minneapolis-St. Paul.

"The marketing margin"

The "marketing margin" is the difference between the price per pound the consumer pays for chicken and the payment the farmer receives for an equivalent quantity of live chicken. About 72 percent of the live chicken reaches the consumer ready to cook. Therefore, the price the farmer receives for approximately 1.4 pounds of live chicken is the equivalent of what the consumer pays for 1 pound of ready-to-cook chicken. The marketing margin includes all charges for procurement, slaughtering, eviscerating, packaging, and distributing chickens. The payment received by the farmer is called the "farm value."

Marketing Costs and Margins for Chicken Fryers and Fowl Sold in Chicago and Minneapolis-St. Paul

By ROBERT M. CONLOGUE, *agricultural economist*, Agricultural Marketing Service

Why and How the Study Was Made

Supplying chicken meat to 170 million consumers is the business of hundreds of thousands of farmers and many marketing firms. In 1956, farmers produced an estimated 4.3 billion pounds of chicken fryers and about 1.7 billion pounds of fowl [1] and other farm chickens. The farm value of this production was over $1 billion.

Consumption of chicken fryers, which has been increasing rapidly since 1934, was nearly 17 pounds per capita, ready-to-cook basis, in 1956 and is continuing to rise. The consumption, as well as the production, of fowl, which has been declining slowly for many years, still was over 7½ pounds per capita. In 1956, total consumption of chicken meat was at the record rate of over 24 pounds per capita.

Marketing a major food item such as chicken meat is complex and involves many costs. The services of many marketing agencies—dealers, processors, transportation companies, warehouses, wholesalers, and retailers—are needed to move chickens from farms to consumers at the times and places and in the forms consumers desire.

Although great strides have been made in improving the efficiency of marketing fryers and fowl in recent years, the total marketing bill for these products may approximate $500 million annually. Many farmers, consumers, and others believe that these charges and the spreads between farm and retail prices are excessive. Marketing firms, on the other hand, generally argue that these marketing costs and margins are reasonable.

This study was undertaken as a result of strong public interest in farm-to-retail price spreads on foods. The purpose of the study and of this report is to provide detailed information on the marketing costs and margins for chicken fryers and fowl sold to consumers in Chicago, Ill., and Minneapolis-St. Paul, Minn.

About 100 representative independent retailers, together with almost a complete representation of chain food store organizations, in each of the 2 urban areas were visited in 1955 and 1956. Information on buying and selling prices and practices was obtained for the 4 months of July and October 1955 and January and April 1956. The questionnaire that was used to obtain information on marketing practices was designed to cover the operations of independent and chain food retailers.

Similar information on buying and selling prices was obtained from the principal wholesalers who

[1] A hen used primarily for laying purposes.

were selling to the retailers in this study and from the processors who were selling to these wholesalers and directly to the retailers. In addition, the wholesalers and processors provided detailed information on their operating costs for each of the 4 months. The processors included not only groups of firms located near each of the 2 metropolitan areas but also about 12 plants in Georgia, Arkansas, and Alabama. During the 4 months, these plants shipped more than 22 million pounds of ready-to-cook fryers to the 2 metropolitan areas.

Gross farm-to-retail price spreads were computed by adding together average margins of the different types of handlers in the particular marketing channels.[2] This method realistically presents the farm-to-retail spread for the total volume handled from farm to retail rather than for any particular segment of that volume, which may or may not, pricewise, be carrying part of the handling costs of other segments.

Costs and Margins

Farm-to-retail price spreads on chicken fryers differ considerably among the forms in which the products are processed and sold, among marketing channels, among stores, and between the two urban areas. These differences are readily explainable on the basis of marketing costs, store pricing policies, and other factors.

Fresh Fryers, Ready to Cook

Average farm-to-retail price spreads on fresh, ready-to-cook fryers in July and October 1955 and January and April 1956 ranged from 15.3 to 21.0 cents a pound in Chicago, and 19.2 to 21.9 cents a pound in Minneapolis-St. Paul (table 1).[3] In Chicago, the total marketing margin was slightly less on fryers processed in nearby plants than on fryers shipped from plants in Arkansas, Georgia, and Alabama. The southern plants included in this study had average margins of 7.7 cents a pound and the nearby processors obtained 6.8 cents a pound. The reverse situation prevailed in the Twin Cities. The nearby processors obtained an average price spread of 9.1 cents a pound, and the southern plants shipping fryers to the Twin Cities had average margins of 8.2 cents a pound.

Generally, during this study, broilers handled by processors in the Minneapolis-St. Paul area were held somewhat longer on the farm than broilers from the Southern States, resulting in a fleshier bird which could be sold at a premium. This involved additional production costs, which were usually covered by the higher price received when sold.

In both metropolitan areas farm-to-retail margins on fresh, ready-to-cook fryers were lower when sold through chainstores than when sold through independent food stores. In Chicago this difference was much greater than in the Twin Cities. The combined margins of Chicago wholesalers and independent retailers averaged 13.3 cents a pound. Margins of Chicago chainstores, performing both the wholesaling and retailing functions, averaged 8.5 cents. The comparable

---

[2] Gross margins of processing plants were computed by subtracting the ready-to-cook equivalent of prices paid to farmers from selling prices received by the plants. The conversion was made by dividing the farm price for live birds by a ready-to-cook yield percentage. For example, a farm price of 18 cents a pound for live birds is equal to 24 cents a pound for ready-to-cook birds, provided that the yield of ready-to-cook poultry meat is 75 percent, or 18 divided by 0.75 equals 24.

[3] See footnote 2.

Type of handler	Average marketing margin for fresh fryers—	
	Sold in Chicago	Sold in Minneapolis-St. Paul
	Cents per pound[1]	Cents per pound[1]
Georgia, Arkansas, and Alabama processors	7.7	8.2
Wholesaler	2.4	2.5
Independent retailer	10.9	10.3
Farm-to-retail	21.0	21.0
Nearby processor [2]	6.8	9.1
Wholesaler	2.4	2.5
Independent retailer	10.9	10.3
Farm-to-retail	20.1	21.9
Georgia, Arkansas, and Alabama processors	7.7	8.2
Chain retailer	8.5	11.0
Farm-to-retail	16.2	19.2
Nearby processor [2]	6.8	9.1
Chain retailer	8.5	11.0
Farm-to-retail	15.3	20.1

[1] Eviscerated weight.
[2] Processing plants within 200 miles of the 2 market areas.

averages in the Twin Cities, as shown in table 1, were 12.8 cents for wholesalers and independents combined, and 11.0 cents for chainstores. For fryers sold through both types of stores, farmers in Georgia, Alabama, and Arkansas received an average of 30 cents per pound (ready-to-cook weight). Farmers near Chicago received 33.3 cents per pound and those in the Minneapolis-St. Paul area received 32.3 cents per pound.

The principal cause of the differences between the average chain store margins in the two urban centers probably is the different retail pricing policies used. In Chicago, fryers were more commonly used by the chains as "specials," or low margin leaders, in the intensive competition among the chains for business. In Minneapolis-St. Paul this sort of competition either was less intense or the chains used products other than fryers as their price leaders to attract customers to their stores.

Average retail prices of fresh eviscerated fryers in independent stores in Chicago ranged from 57.5 cents a pound in July 1955 to 47.8 cents a pound in April 1956. In Minneapolis-St. Paul the range in independent stores was 56.7 cents a pound in July 1955 to 47.9 cents a pound in April 1956. Average chainstore prices in Chicago ranged from 56.7 cents a pound in July 1955 to 44.7 cents a pound in April 1956, and in Minneapolis-St. Paul 59.6

cents a pound in July 1955 to 45.9 cents a pound in April 1956.

On the basis of these figures, farmers received about 59 percent of the consumer's dollar for ice-packed fryers moving through independent retailers, 62½ percent for these fryers moving through Minneapolis-St. Paul chains, and 68 percent when moving through Chicago chains. These varying percentages are more the result of variations in retail prices than of farm prices since the average price received by Georgia, Arkansas, and Alabama farmers was 30 cents per pound, ready-to-cook weight, for fryers sold through both independent and chain retailers during this period. Processors nearby Chicago averaged 32.8 cents per pound, nearby Minneapolis-St. Paul, 31.1 cents per pound, ready-to-cook weight, during the same period.

Detailed price data on fresh fryers, ready-to-cook, are presented in appendix tables 5-7 and in figure 1.

Operating cost data were secured from each of the cooperating processors and wholesalers to determine the component parts of average margins for each type of distributor. For Georgia, Arkansas, and Alabama processors, operating costs averaged 6.75 cents a pound, eviscerated weight, and for nearby processors, 7.80 cents a pound. The net operating return to capital and management was 0.95 cent a pound for the southern processors, representing profit before taxes and a reserve for less profitable periods, and 0.15 cent a pound for nearby processors (table 2).

Wholesalers' operating costs totaled 2.40 cents a pound, leaving a net operating return of 0.05 cent. Their costs were as follows:

	Cents per pound[1]
Salaries and wages	1.54
Building, including fuel, power, and light	.21
Transportation	.21
Soliciting and selling	.16

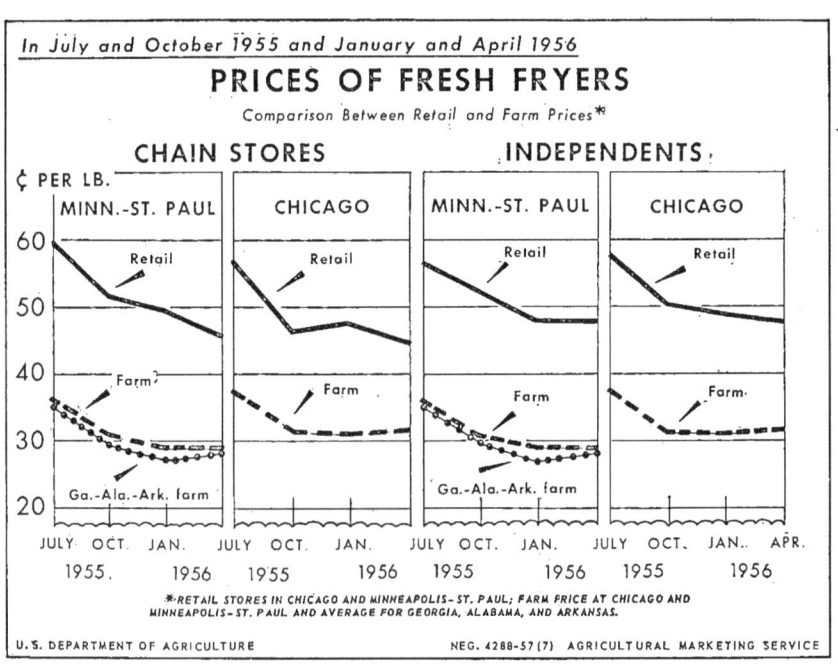

FIGURE 1.

	Cents per pound[1]
Interest, bank charges, bank accounts, etc	0.02
Office supplies, accounting, etc	.08
Overhead	.18
Total operating costs	2.40
Gross margin	2.45
Net operating return	.05

[1] Eviscerated weight.

Frozen Fryers

Average farm-to-retail price spreads on frozen fryers ranged from 27.5 to 41.4 cents a pound in Chicago and 33.2 to 41.1 cents a pound in Minneapolis-St. Paul (table 3). In both areas the total margin was about 5 cents a pound lower on frozen fryers from southern plants than on frozen fryers from frozen food processors. Margins of the southern processors averaged 17.4 cents a pound and of the frozen food processors, 22.6 cents a pound. In Chicago the farm-to-retail price spread was lower on frozen fryers sold through chainstores than on those sold through independent retail stores. The combined margins of wholesalers and independent retailers handling frozen fryers was about 19 cents a pound in both Chicago and the Twin Cities. Chainstores performing both the wholesaling and retailing function had average margins of 10.3 cents a pound in Chicago and 15.5 cents a pound in Minneapolis-St. Paul.

The differences in margins on frozen fryers may be explained by the differences in organization of the specialty processor and the frozen food processor and the different pricing policies used by both the processors and the chains.

Most of the frozen fryers shipped by the southern processors into retail channels were sold to chainstores or large supermarkets in truckload lots. Some were shipped as whole fryers and were either cut

TABLE 2.—*Broilers and fresh fowl: Operating costs, including overhead and profit or loss, of processors near Chicago and Minneapolis-St. Paul and of processors in Georgia, Arkansas, and Alabama, July and October 1955 and January and April 1956*

	Cost per pound (eviscerated weight)	
Item	Southern processors[1]	Nearby processors[2]
	Cents	Cents
Hauling (farm to plant)	0.90	0.60
Labor (receiving, dressing, packaging)	2.00	3.00
Dressing costs, other than labor	1.00	1.05
Packaging costs, other than labor	.95	1.05
Delivery (plant to consuming area)	.85	.85
Overhead	1.05	1.25
Total operating costs	6.75	7.80
Gross margin	7.70	7.95
Net operating return	[3].95	[3].15

[1] Processors of icepacked broilers in Georgia, Arkansas, and Alabama.
[2] Processors of broilers and fresh fowl within a 200-mile radius of Chicago and Minneapolis-St. Paul.
[3] Net operating return to capital and management for 4 months represented profit before taxes and a reserve for less profitable periods.

TABLE 3.—*Fryers, frozen: Typical farm-to-retail marketing margins by various marketing channels, 1955–56*

Type of handler	Average marketing margin for frozen fryers—	
	Sold in Chicago	Sold in Minneapolis-St. Paul
	Cents per pound [1]	*Cents per pound* [1]
Frozen food distributor-processor	22.4	22.9
Wholesaler	5.9	3.9
Independent retailer	13.1	14.3
Farm-to-retail	41.4	41.1
Georgia, Arkansas, and Alabama processors	17.2	17.7
Chain retailer	10.3	15.5
Farm-to-retail	27.5	33.2

[1] Eviscerated weight.

up before shipping or were thawed later and cut up and retailed in unfrozen form. Some were packed as individual parts.

The frozen food processors covered by this study are differentiated from the specialty processors in that the frozen food processors distribute numerous frozen food items of which poultry is only a relatively minor one. These frozen food distributors ordinarily have division offices in all of the larger cities, branch offices in the smaller cities, and salesmen covering areas in which the smallest cities, towns, and villages are located. This wide coverage of retail outlets makes their products available to all consumers wherever they live, but distribution costs are heavy. Nearly every retail food store has a frozen food box, which is replenished weekly or monthly by frozen food distributors using refrigerated delivery trucks. Throughout the country, thousands of retail food stores that are not equipped to handle fresh poultry have frozen food boxes in which they carry small quantities of frozen whole cut-up chicken or chicken parts. For these stores the cost of marketing is necessarily high; consequently the farm-to-consumer price spread is much wider than for large volume retail handlers.

In chainstores about the same situation prevailed for frozen fryers as for fresh fryers. Chains in Chicago were operating on lower margins than chains in Minneapolis-St. Paul because of intensive competition. Average chainstore prices of frozen eviscerated fryers in Chicago ranged from 61.7 cents a pound in July 1955 to 48.8 cents a pound in April 1956, and in Minneapolis-St. Paul from 69.5 cents a pound in July 1955 to 59.5 cents a pound in January 1956. Data on chains in Minneapolis-St. Paul were not available for April 1956. Average retail prices of frozen eviscerated fryers in independent stores in Chicago ranged from 75.4 cents a pound in July 1955 to 67.8 cents a pound in April 1956. In Minneapolis-St. Paul the range in independent stores was from 74.0 cents a pound in July 1955 to 65.6 cents a pound in April 1956. Detailed price data for frozen fryers are given in appendix tables 8 and 9.

Operating costs for Georgia, Arkansas, and Alabama processors of frozen fryers averaged 17.23 cents a pound and the net operating return was 0.22 cent. The costs consisted of—

	Cents a pound [1]
Hauling (farm to plant)	1.06
Labor (receiving, dressing, packaging)	4.04
Dressing costs, other than labor	.96
Packaging costs, other than labor	2.32
Freezing	.50
Ice	.20
Plant overhead	2.34
Administration	.59
Miscellaneous	.25
Delivery	2.44
Storage	.60
Commissions (selling)	.50
Advertising	1.43
Total operating costs	17.23
Gross margin	17.45
Net operating return	.22

[1] Eviscerated weight.

Frozen food processors' operating costs averaged 18.30 cents a pound. An additional 4.10 cents a pound, for which specific costs are not shown in the following tabulation, is included in the gross margin. This margin may cover some distribution and selling costs as well as profits in marketing frozen poultry and other frozen foods. Or, poultry may be carrying part of the marketing costs of one or more other frozen foods more competitive than poultry but processed by the same companies. Insofar as we were able to determine, there are no wholesalers, as such, who handle frozen poultry exclusively. The following is a breakdown of the operating costs of frozen food processors:

	Cents a pound [1]
Hauling (farm to plant)	0.45
Receiving and feeding	.30
Killing and dressing	.45
Eviscerating	1.35
Cutting up	.30
Froster labor	.30
Packing labor	1.35
Packaging materials	2.55
Manufacturing overhead and other miscellaneous	6.20
Storage and transportation	3.05
Selling and advertising	1.40
General administrative	.30
Other	.30
Total operating costs, including overhead	18.30
Other distributive costs interwoven with distribution costs of frozen foods other than poultry	4.10
Total operating and distribution costs including overhead and profit or loss	22.40

[1] Eviscerated weight.

Since frozen food distributors and buying organizations of voluntary chains buy from processors and sell to retailers or institutions, data on prices paid and prices received were recorded for them as wholesalers of frozen poultry. No attempt was made to collect operating cost data for these firms because of the impossibility of allocating to poultry the common costs for hundreds of frozen food items.

Markups on frozen poultry by frozen food distributors are determined in various ways. In a number of firms frozen poultry was placed in a certain category with many other frozen foods and the same markup applied to all foods in that category. In other firms, the markup varied depending on whether the item was whole frozen, whole cut-up, or individual parts. In some firms the markup varied depending on whether the frozen poultry was shipped directly from the processing plant or shipped from a storage warehouse of the processing firm.

Differences in markups between poultry direct from the production line and that from the processor's warehouse were caused by the differences in prices paid by frozen food distributors, since selling prices were the same. At times warehouse prices were 7 cents a pound higher

7

than prices of poultry direct from the production line. At other times the warehouse price was about the same or only slightly higher. One explanation of the higher warehouse price was that small stores bought in small quantities requiring expensive handling and delivery in the warehouse, whereas large buyers bought in carload lots direct from the processing plants. The large buyers paid lower prices because of lower unit costs, involving no warehousing by the processor and much lower handling and transportation costs.

The method for distributing frozen poultry in both Chicago and Minneapolis-St. Paul differs considerably between chains and independents. Chains, with their generally large units, handle both fresh and frozen poultry so that consumers have a choice of either. On the other hand, most of the small independents do not have facilities for handling fresh poultry, but they do keep frozen poultry. For the most part, independents, except the large ones, keep their poultry in frozen food boxes. As the boxes are also used for other types of frozen foods, space is at a premium; thus only small quantities are kept on hand. These independents rely on frozen food distributors to keep the frozen food box supplied, which is of necessity an expensive method of distribution, requiring frequent deliveries of small quantities. Consequently, prices are high. In contrast, chainstores with their heavy volume and generally better facilities purchase from large independent poultry processors at considerably lower prices.

It is interesting to note the disparity between the prices of fresh and frozen poultry. According to data on processing costs, the cost of processing and freezing poultry is only slightly higher than the cost of processing fresh ice-packed poultry, but apparently accrual of costs after processing and freezing leads to the much higher price level. This phase of the distribution and marketing of frozen poultry has been selected for further study.

Fresh Fowl

Average farm-to-retail price spreads on fresh fowl ranged from 17.3 cents to 22.8 cents a pound (table 4). In Chicago, the the total marketing margin was about 3 cents a pound less when fowl was marketed through chains than when it was marketed through wholesalers and independent stores; but in Minneapolis the total margin was about 1½ cents a pound higher when fowl moved through chains. Competition in Chicago seemed to be somewhat more pressing than in Minneapolis-St. Paul, particularly in chainstores. In addition, in the Minneapolis-St. Paul area, store policy resulted in higher margins on fowl in chainstores than in independent stores.

Operating costs for fresh fowl were about the same as for fresh fryers.

New York dressed fowl were handled by relatively few retailers in Minneapolis and St. Paul. The farm-to-retail price spread averaged 18.2 cents a pound (table 4). The following tabulation shows the operating costs for local processors of New York dressed fowl:

Cents a pound[1]

Hauling (farm to plant)	0.38
Feeding	.39
Materials and supplies	.49
Dressing labor	2.24
Overhead	2.00
Other	2.14
Total operating costs, including overhead	7.64
Gross margin	9.50
Net operating return	1.86

[1] New York dressed weight.

Average retail prices of fresh eviscerated fowl in independent stores in Chicago ranged from 52.6 cents a pound in October 1955 to

TABLE 4.—*Fowl, fresh, New York dressed, and frozen: Typical farm-to-retail marketing margins by various marketing channels, 1955–56*

Commodity and type of handler	Average marketing margin of fowl—	
	Sold in Chicago	Sold in Minneapolis-St. Paul
	Cents per pound [1]	Cents per pound [1]
Fowl, fresh:		
Nearby processor [2]	7.0	8.5
Wholesaler	3.7	3.7
Independent retailer	9.7	9.0
Farm-to-retail	20.4	21.2
Nearby processor	7.0	8.5
Chain retailer	10.3	14.3
Farm-to-retail	17.3	22.8
Fowl, New York dressed:		
Nearby processor		[3] 9.5
Independent retailer		[3] 8.7
Farm-to-retail		[3] 18.2
Fowl, frozen:		
Georgia, Arkansas, and Alabama processors	12.9	
Chain retailer	10.1	
Farm-to-retail	23.0	

[1] Eviscerated weight.
[2] Processing plants within 200 miles of consuming area.
[3] New York dressed weight.

46.9 cents a pound in January 1956. In Minneapolis-St. Paul the range in independent stores was 46.4 cents a pound in January 1956 to 51.0 cents in April 1956. Average chainstore prices in Chicago ranged from 48.1 cents a pound in October 1955 to 48.9 cents in January 1956 and in Minneapolis-St. Paul, 49.7 cents a pound in July 1955 to 55.9 cents in April 1956. Detailed price data on fresh fowl, roasters, and capons and caponettes, ready to cook, are presented in tables 10–13 in the appendix.

Frozen Fowl

The average farm-to-retail price spread on frozen fowl was 23 cents a pound (table 4). Sufficient usable data on this item were available only for Georgia, Alabama, and Arkansas processors selling through chainstores. Average chainstore prices of frozen eviscerated fowl in Chicago ranged from 50.7 cents a pound in July 1955 to 49.4 cents a pound in April 1956 (appendix table 14).

Operating costs for processors of frozen fowl were about the same as for processors of frozen fryers.

Marketing Practices

Generally, it was found that the average small independent retailer plans from day to day, whereas the larger chain and independent stores may plan their operations weeks, months, and even years in advance.

Advertising

Questions on advertising policy elicited rather specific replies from the larger operators, but generally vague replies from most of the small operators. In some cases, particularly in the Minneapolis-St. Paul area where voluntary chains (wholesaler-retailer membership groups) are important factors in food distribution, advertising was done by wholesalers for their member retailers. Overall advertising followed the pattern shown below:

MEDIA USED

Percentage of total number of independent retailers

Minneapolis-St.	News-papers	Radio	Hand-bills	None
Paul	40	0	15	45
Chicago	20	2	22	56

Only about 16 percent of all independent retailers included in the study advertised weekly. The rest of the advertising depended upon numerous circumstances, such as market conditions, competitors' advertising, the price of red meats, and seasonal changes. Most of the advertising was on weekends or on days prior to holidays. Generally, poultry was advertised along with other commodities.

Reaction to the effects of advertising was mixed. Some store owners or operators, even of the larger stores, were not sure that they gained by advertising. Some of them indicated that they had enough regular customers who would buy from day to day in their stores regardless of advertised sales and that the sales benefited itinerant trade actually at the expense of regular customers since they said income lost on sales of poultry had to be made up on sales of other commodities. This seems to be one of the important problems the independent retailers face since they lack the capital to carry on extended advertising campaigns designed to draw customers away from, or even to hold regular customers from changing to, the larger chainstore or independent outlets.

Two rather specific changes in independent retailing have taken place: (1) The number of small independent stores has declined and in many cases has been replaced by large multiple-unit supermarkets comparable to the largest units of competing chains. This type of operation necessarily requires capital running into tens of thousands of dollars and therefore puts it out of reach of the corner grocery store owner. (2) Owners of small neighborhood stores have more and more tended to handle convenience items, no longer selling fresh meats, fresh poultry, or fresh vegetables. They have also resorted to remaining open long hours at night and, where possible, holidays and Sundays, when their larger competitors are closed. They have extended credit heavily to customers who prefer to buy on credit. A number of the small independent retailers said that they were being "squeezed" out of business.

Determination of Purchase Price and Selling Price

Questions on determination of purchase price and selling price elicited fairly standard replies. Nearly all paid the asking price of regular suppliers. Few shopped around. About 75 percent said they used a customary percentage markup, established over the years, in determining the selling price. Others used a customary cents-per-pound markup, and still others, particularly the large independents, followed chainstore competitive prices.

Surplus Stocks

Surplus stocks were no problem since leftovers were ether frozen and stored or packed in ice and stored in coolers for future sale. There was little waste or spoilage except in a few instances where the retailers cut-up poultry and had difficulty disposing of backs and necks.

Markings on Displays

About half of the retailers price-tagged poultry, and only about one-third used any nomenclature on displays. These ran the gamut of the field, such as heavy hens, light hens, young fryers, fancy springs, and tender home-grown chickens.

Refrigeration

About half of the stores in Minneapolis-St. Paul and two-thirds of those in Chicago used walk-in coolers and refrigerated display cases, enabling them to handle fresh poultry. Most of these and nearly all of the others had freezers or frozen food cases where they kept frozen poultry.

Deliveries to Stores

Deliveries varied from daily to once or twice a week for fresh poultry to once a week or once every 2 months for frozen poultry. Most deliveries were made in refrigerated trucks during the morning or early afternoon.

Related Information

Handlers of Live Poultry

The once prevalent method of distributing live poultry to city retail markets has almost disappeared. Many laws and regulations either prohibit the practice altogether or establish requirements which are too expensive for a retailer to follow. However, in and near Minneapolis-St. Paul there are still a few live poultry handlers who pick up poultry, mostly fowl, at farms and deliver the poultry to processing plants located within the area. Some of these handlers originally operated small dressing plants of their own—generally old-fashioned hand operations where fowl were New York dressed and delivered to stores in a nearby large city. Increasing labor costs, resulting from job opportunities in other industries, and constantly increasing competition from more efficiently organized commercial plants reduced margins, necessitating a change. Former small processors found it advisable to remain in the poultry business, using their trucks to pick up fowl at farms and deliver them live to processing plants. Two principal methods were used: (1) The handler purchased the fowl outright and sold them to processors or canners; and (2) the processor or canner paid the producer for the fowl and paid the handler for pickup and hauling.

Handlers had an average gross margin of about 2½ cents a pound when they purchased outright from the farmer. When the processor or canner paid the producer and then paid the handler for pickup and delivery, the handler generally received 3 cents a pound for pickup at the farm, including delivery to the plant, and 1 cent a pound for fowl picked up from dealers. Dealers, generally located in small towns, acted as a first handler for live poultry, either picking up at the farm or accepting deliveries from farmers and holding for the trucker. These dealers ordinarily had other enterprises, such as handling feed, eggs, and farm equipment. They operated on margins of 1 to 2 cents a pound, thus making the total margin on live poultry from 2 to 3 cents a pound. These margins covered the cost of trucks, gasoline and oil, repairs, drivers, and in some cases, helpers. Net margins were small, since volume per operator generally was low. These dealers quite often used their trucks for many purposes other than assembling chickens.

Location of Concentrated Broiler-Producing Areas

The largest areas of broiler production are located in the southern and eastern sections of the United States. Smaller but important areas are also found in California, Texas, Indiana, some of the other Midwestern States, and the Northwestern States. The 1954 Census of Agriculture listed Georgia, with 114.4 million broilers, as the leading State in number of broilers sold. Next in order in sales of millions of broilers were Arkansas, 62.3; Delaware, 61.6; Texas, 55.7; Maryland, 46.1; Alabama, 39.6; California, 38.3; Virginia, 37.0; North Carolina, 35.5; and Mississippi, 34.4. Several other States, including Indiana, Pennsylvania, Maine, Missouri, West Virginia, and Connecticut, sold broilers in amounts ranging from 15 to 28½ million. The heaviest producing counties are shown in appendix table 15.

Distribution of Broilers to Consuming Areas

Broilers produced along the eastern seaboard are nearly all consumed in cities located in the East; outshipments are few. Shipments into New York City, during 1955, were heaviest from Maine, Maryland, and Delaware. Philadelphia purchased heavily from Delaware and Maryland. Boston received most of its broilers from Maine, and other cities in the East had similar patterns. Broilers produced in the Southern States are shipped to nearly all sections of the United States. Shipments into the eastern seaboard cities are relatively light, however, partly because of the competition from nearby areas. As an indication of the distribution pattern, Georgia ships heavily to such widely scattered cities as Pittsburgh, Cleveland, Detroit, Chicago, Cincinnati, and Los Angeles. Data on shipments from heavy producing

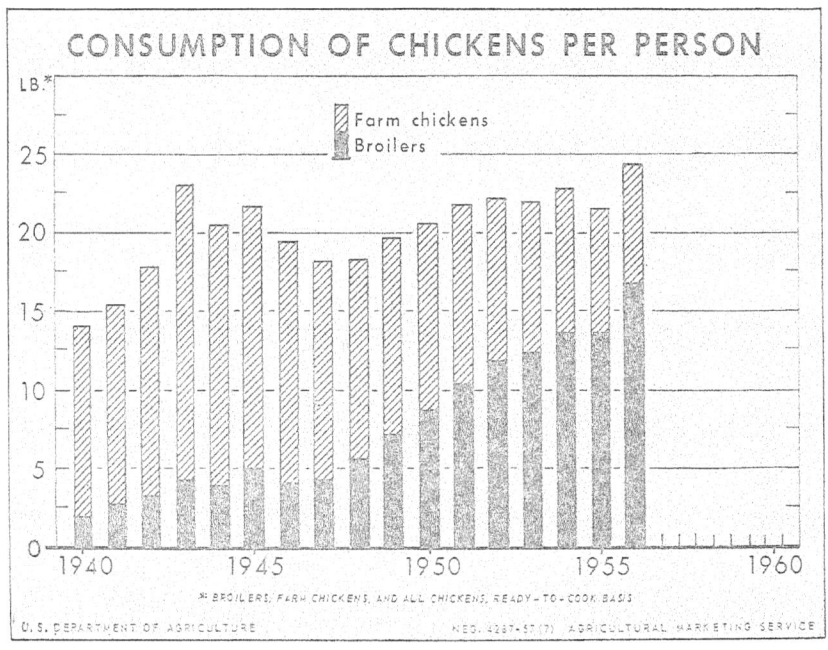

Figure 2.

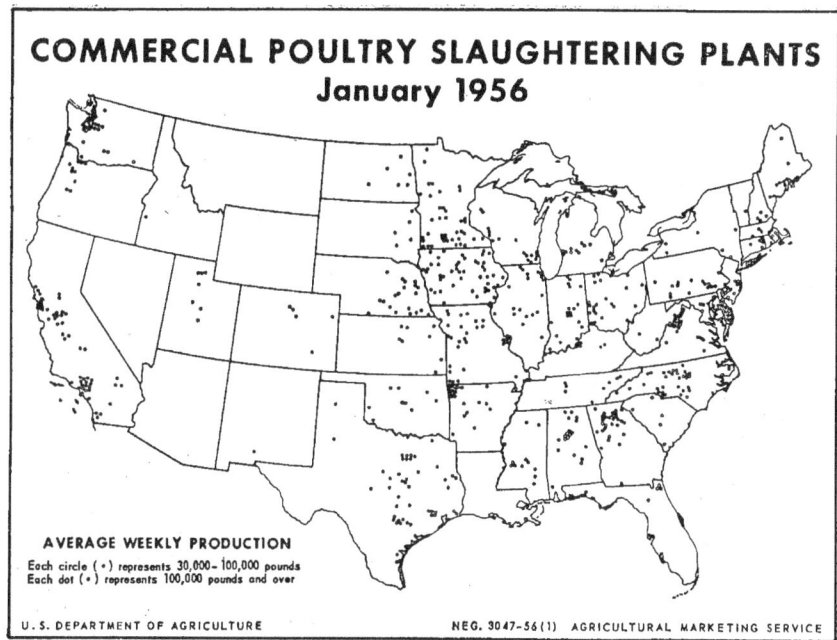

FIGURE 3.

areas to important consumption areas are shown in appendix table 16.

Per Capita Consumption

Chicken fryers or broilers have come into their own in recent years as a frequently recurring dish on the average American table. In 1940, per capita consumption of broilers was about 2 pounds. In 1956 per capita consumption exceeded 16 pounds. This rapid increase in per capita consumption of broilers was partly due to a decline in the production of farm chickens, per capita consumption of which dropped from 12 pounds in 1940 to about 7 pounds in 1956. During this period per capita consumption of all chickens increased from 14 pounds to 24 (fig. 2 and appendix table 17).

Prices of chicken in comparison with other meats have had much to do with the increase in use of chicken over the past few years. This decline in comparative prices was due in large part to the commercialization of the industry. Production in mass numbers enabled producers to develop more efficient methods, better quality in general, and to educate the general public through extensive advertising.

Location of Processing Plants

The location of processing or slaughtering plants in relation to heavy consuming areas indicates in a broad sense the task involved in moving a highly perishable commodity long distances. Figure 3 shows the location of poultry slaughtering plants and also indicates the density of poultry production since these plants are usually located in the producing areas.

Appendix

List of Tables

Table No.		Page
5	Fryers, fresh (eviscerated): Average selling price, purchase cost, and margin, by type of handler, July and October 1955, January and April 1956, and 4-month averages	15
6	Fryers, fresh (purchased whole, sold cut up): Average selling price, purchase cost, and margin, Chicago independent retailers, July and October 1955, January and April 1956, and 4-month averages	16
7	Chicken parts, fresh: Average selling price, purchase cost, and margin, Chicago independent retailers, July and October 1955, January and April 1956, and 4-month averages	17
8	Fryers, frozen (eviscerated): Average selling price, purchase cost, and margin, by type of handler, July and October 1955, January and April 1956, and 4-month averages	18
9	Chicken parts, frozen: Average selling price, purchase cost, and margin, by type of handler, July and October 1955, January and April 1956, and 4-month averages	20
10	Fowl, fresh (eviscerated): Average selling price, purchase cost, and margin, by type of handler, July and October 1955, January and April 1956, and 4-month averages	26
11	Fowl, New York dressed: Average selling price, purchase cost, and margin, by type of handler, July and October 1955, January and April 1956, and 4-month averages	27
12	Roasters, fresh: Average selling price, purchase cost, and margin, by type of handler, July and October 1955, January and April 1956, and 4-month averages	28
13	Capons and caponettes, fresh: Average selling price, purchase cost, and margin, Chicago independent retailers, July and October 1955, January and April 1956, and 4-month averages	28
14	Fowl, frozen (eviscerated): Average selling price, purchase cost, and margin, by type of handler, July and October 1955, January and April 1956, and 4-month averages	29
15	Broilers: Number and value sold in 20 leading counties, 1954	29
16	Poultry: Number of broilers sold from certain States, 1954, and amount of processed poultry received at various markets, by State of origin, 1955	30
17	Civilian per capita consumption: Broilers, farm chickens, and all chickens, ready-to-cook basis, 1940–56	31

TABLE 5.—*Fryers, fresh (eviscerated): Average selling price, purchase cost, and margin, by type of handler, July and October 1955, January and April 1956, and 4-month averages*

Outlet, month, and year	Average selling price per pound	Average purchase cost per pound	Average margin per pound
Georgia, Alabama, and Arkansas processors:			
Chicago:	Cents	Cents	Cents
July 1955	43.1	35.2	7.9
October 1955	37.5	29.7	7.8
January 1956	34.4	27.0	7.4
April 1956	35.7	28.1	7.6
4-month average	37.7	30.0	7.7
Minneapolis-St. Paul:			
July 1955	43.6	35.2	8.4
October 1955	38.0	29.7	8.3
January 1956	34.9	27.0	7.9
April 1956	36.2	28.1	8.1
4-month average	38.2	30.0	8.2
Nearby processors:			
Chicago:			
July 1955	45.4	37.1	8.3
October 1955	37.8	31.2	6.6
January 1956	37.8	31.0	6.8
April 1956	37.5	31.7	5.8
4-month average	39.6	32.8	6.8
Minneapolis-St. Paul:			
July 1955	45.0	35.8	9.2
October 1955	39.7	30.9	8.8
January 1956	37.5	29.0	8.5
April 1956	38.7	28.7	10.0
4-month average	40.2	31.1	9.1
Wholesalers:			
Chicago:			
July 1955	45.5	42.8	2.7
October 1955	38.4	36.0	2.4
January 1956	37.2	34.7	2.5
April 1956	37.4	35.4	2.0
4-month average	39.6	37.2	2.4
Minneapolis-St. Paul:			
July 1955	47.4	44.7	2.7
October 1955	40.5	38.0	2.5
January 1956	39.0	36.6	2.4
April 1956	38.5	36.3	2.2
4-month average	41.4	38.9	2.5

TABLE 5.—*Fryers, fresh (eviscerated): Average selling price, purchase cost, and margin, by type of handler, July and October 1955, January and April 1956, and 4-month averages*—Continued

Outlet, month, and year	Average selling price per pound	Average purchase cost per pound	Average margin per pound
	Cents	Cents	Cents
Independent retailers:			
Chicago:			
July 1955	57.5	46.1	11.4
October 1955	50.1	40.1	10.0
January 1956	48.8	37.3	11.5
April 1956	47.8	37.3	10.5
4-month average	51.1	40.2	10.9
Minneapolis-St. Paul:			
July 1955	56.7	46.5	10.2
October 1955	52.3	40.9	11.4
January 1956	48.0	38.5	9.5
April 1956	47.9	37.7	10.2
4-month average	51.2	40.9	10.3
Chain retailers:			
Chicago:			
July 1955	56.7	47.1	9.6
October 1955	46.4	39.7	6.7
January 1956	47.4	37.5	9.9
April 1956	44.7	36.8	7.9
4-month average	48.8	40.3	8.5
Minneapolis-St. Paul:			
July 1955	59.6	47.2	12.4
October 1955	51.9	39.2	12.7
January 1956	49.6	38.8	10.8
April 1956	45.9	38.0	7.9
4-month average	51.8	40.8	11.0

TABLE 6.—*Fryers, fresh (purchased whole, sold cut up): Average selling price, purchase cost, and margin, Chicago independent retailers, July and October 1955, January and April 1956, and 4-month averages*

Outlet, month, and year	Average selling price per pound	Average purchase cost per pound	Average margin per pound
	Cents	Cents	Cents
July 1955	54.3	41.1	13.2
October 1955	58.9	39.1	19.8
January 1956	52.2	37.7	14.5
April 1956	52.6	35.4	17.2
4-month average	54.5	38.3	16.2

TABLE 7.—*Chicken parts, fresh: Average selling price, purchase cost, and margin, Chicago independent retailers, July and October 1955, January and April 1956, and 4-month averages*

Part of chicken and date	Average selling price per pound	Average purchase cost per pound	Average margin per pound
Breasts:	*Cents*	*Cents*	*Cents*
July 1955	88.9	72.4	16.5
October 1955	88.1	71.2	16.9
January 1956	81.5	63.7	17.8
April 1956	83.1	63.3	19.8
4-month average	85.4	67.6	17.8
Legs:			
July 1955	82.1	65.4	16.7
October 1955	79.7	63.4	16.3
January 1956	70.7	55.0	15.7
April 1956	71.1	55.2	15.9
4-month average	75.9	59.8	16.1
Wings:			
July 1955	46.6	31.1	15.5
October 1955	42.5	31.2	11.3
January 1956	39.0	29.1	9.9
April 1956	46.2	30.0	16.2
4-month average	43.6	30.4	13.2
Necks and backs:			
July 1955	10.0	5.9	4.1
October 1955	10.1	5.5	4.6
January 1956	10.1	5.6	4.5
April 1956	10.0	3.9	6.1
4-month average	10.0	5.2	4.8

TABLE 8.—*Fryers, frozen (eviscerated): Average selling price, purchase cost, and margin by type of handler, July and October 1955, January and April 1956, and 4-month averages*

Outlet, month, and year	Average selling price per pound	Average purchase cost per pound	Average margin per pound
Georgia, Alabama, and Arkansas processors:	*Cents*	*Cents*	*Cents*
Chicago:			
July 1955	53.0	36.7	16.3
October 1955	47.6	29.7	17.9
January 1956	45.5	28.7	16.8
April 1956	46.8	29.1	17.7
4-month average	48.2	31.0	17.2
Minneapolis-St. Paul:			
July 1955	53.5	36.7	16.8
October 1955	48.1	29.7	18.4
January 1956	46.0	28.7	17.3
April 1956	47.3	29.1	18.2
4-month average	48.7	31.0	17.7
Frozen food distributors:			
Chicago:			
July 1955	55.6	38.6	17.0
October 1955	57.3	29.2	28.1
January 1956	51.2	28.5	22.7
April 1956	49.5	27.6	21.9
4-month average	53.4	31.0	22.4
Minneapolis-St. Paul:			
July 1955	56.1	38.6	17.5
October 1955	57.8	29.2	28.6
January 1956	51.7	28.5	23.2
April 1956	50.0	27.6	22.4
4-month average	53.9	31.0	22.9
Wholesalers:			
Chicago:			
July 1955	60.7	55.5	5.2
October 1955	59.2	53.9	5.3
January 1956	54.9	48.9	6.0
April 1956	54.8	47.5	7.3
4-month average	57.4	51.5	5.9
Minneapolis-St. Paul:			
July 1955	60.3	56.6	3.7
October 1955	57.3	53.8	3.5
January 1956	48.5	45.5	3.0
April 1956	51.9	46.5	5.4
4-month average	54.5	50.6	3.9

TABLE 8.—*Fryers, frozen (eviserated): Average selling price, purchase cost, and margin by type of handler, July and October 1955, January and April 1956, 4-month averages*—Continued

Outlet, month, and year	Average selling price per pound	Average purchase cost per pound	Average margin per pound
Independent retailers:	*Cents*	*Cents*	*Cents*
Chicago:			
July 1955	75.4	62.4	13.0
October 1955	76.3	62.9	13.4
January 1956	68.2	56.4	11.8
April 1956	67.8	53.5	14.3
4-month average	71.9	58.8	13.1
Minneapolis-St. Paul:			
July 1955	74.0	60.4	13.6
October 1955	70.9	56.0	14.9
January 1956	67.4	53.0	14.4
April 1956	65.6	51.3	14.3
4-month average	69.5	55.2	14.3
Chain retailers:			
Chicago:			
July 1955	61.7	49.6	12.1
October 1955	59.9	49.1	10.8
January 1956	55.8	45.4	10.4
April 1956	48.8	41.0	7.8
4-month average	56.6	46.3	10.3
Minneapolis-St. Paul:			
July 1955	69.5	54.0	15.5
October 1955	62.5	47.0	15.5
January 1956	59.5	44.0	15.5
April 1956	(¹)	(¹)	(¹)
3-month average	63.8	48.3	15.5

¹ Not available.

TABLE 9.—*Chicken parts, frozen: Average selling price, purchase cost, and margin, by type of handler, July and October 1955, January and April 1956, and 4-month averages*

BREASTS

Outlet, month, and year	Average selling price per pound	Average purchase cost per pound	Average margin per pound
Wholesalers:			
Chicago:	*Cents*	*Cents*	*Cents*
July 1955	96.0	86.6	9.4
October 1955	103.4	94.4	9.0
January 1956	101.9	92.9	9.0
April 1956	99.5	89.0	10.5
4-month average	100.2	90.7	9.5
Minneapolis-St. Paul:			
July 1955	97.0	90.8	6.2
October 1955	100.1	93.4	6.7
January 1956	102.2	95.5	6.7
April 1956	100.3	93.2	7.1
4-month average	99.9	93.2	6.7
Independent retailers:			
Chicago:			
July 1955	113.6	92.1	21.5
October 1955	112.2	91.5	20.7
January 1956	110.5	92.7	17.8
April 1956	111.1	93.4	17.7
4-month average	111.8	92.4	19.4
Minneapolis-St. Paul:			
July 1955	110.1	94.7	15.4
October 1955	113.8	97.1	16.7
January 1956	114.2	97.2	17.0
April 1956	113.5	95.2	18.3
4-month average	112.9	96.1	16.8
Chain retailers:			
Chicago:			
July 1955	109.0	82.0	27.0
October 1955	109.0	83.6	25.4
January 1956	108.9	82.4	26.5
April 1956	105.1	83.6	21.5
4-month average	108.0	82.9	25.1
Minneapolis-St. Paul:			
July 1955	112.8	89.6	23.2
October 1955	117.5	95.4	22.1
January 1956	100.0	75.3	24.7
April 1956	(¹)	(¹)	(¹)
3-month average	110.1	86.8	23.3

¹ Not available.

TABLE 9.—*Chicken parts, frozen: Average selling price, purchase cost, and margin, by type of handler, July and October 1955, January and April 1956, and 4-month averages*—Continued

LEGS

Outlet, month, and year	Average selling price per pound	Average purchase cost per pound	Average margin per pound
Wholesalers:			
Chicago:	Cents	Cents	Cents
July 1955	92.4	83.2	9.2
October 1955	90.3	79.0	11.3
January 1956	87.6	76.4	11.2
April 1956	84.9	72.1	12.8
4-month average	88.8	77.7	11.1
Minneapolis-St. Paul:			
July 1955	91.0	83.9	7.1
October 1955	86.0	79.1	6.9
January 1956	82.5	76.5	6.0
April 1956	72.1	66.5	5.6
4-month average	82.9	76.5	6.4
Independent retailers:			
Chicago:			
July 1955	108.4	90.6	17.8
October 1955	108.0	88.3	19.7
January 1956	106.4	87.3	19.1
April 1956	105.8	86.4	19.4
4-month average	107.2	88.2	19.0
Minneapolis-St. Paul:			
July 1955	107.8	88.3	19.5
October 1955	106.5	86.8	19.7
January 1956	102.6	82.8	19.8
April 1956	96.6	77.3	19.3
4-month average	103.4	83.8	19.6
Chain retailers:			
Chicago:			
July 1955	98.0	68.0	30.0
October 1955	98.0	71.2	26.8
January 1956	97.5	63.2	34.3
April 1956	91.1	64.4	26.7
4-month average	96.2	66.7	29.5
Minneapolis-St. Paul:			
July 1955	95.7	74.9	20.8
October 1955	95.0	72.0	23.0
January 1956	82.4	64.8	17.6
April 1956	(¹)	(¹)	(¹)
3-month average	91.0	70.6	20.5

[1] Not available.

TABLE 9.—*Chicken parts, frozen: Average selling price, purchase cost, and margin, by type of handler, July and October 1955, January and April 1956, and 4-month averages*—Continued

THIGHS

Outlet, month, and year	Average selling price per pound	Average purchase cost per pound	Average margin per pound
Wholesalers:			
Chicago:	*Cents*	*Cents*	*Cents*
July 1955	78.1	69.6	8.5
October 1955	78.7	69.4	9.3
January 1956	77.3	67.7	9.6
April 1956	71.4	64.4	7.0
4-month average	76.4	67.8	8.6
Minneapolis-St. Paul:			
July 1955	78.1	71.6	6.5
October 1955	74.3	69.2	5.1
January 1956	70.6	65.8	4.8
April 1956	73.0	68.3	4.7
4-month average	74.0	68.7	5.3
Independent retailers:			
Chicago:			
July 1955	102.5	82.7	19.8
October 1955	104.8	85.2	19.6
January 1956	96.9	80.5	16.4
April 1956	97.1	79.1	18.0
4-month average	100.3	81.9	18.4
Minneapolis-St. Paul:			
July 1955	98.4	80.4	17.8
October 1955	98.0	80.2	17.8
January 1956	92.4	74.2	18.2
April 1956	93.8	77.3	16.5
4-month average	95.6	78.0	17.6
Chain retailers:			
Minneapolis-St. Paul:			
July 1955	93.7	69.2	24.5
October 1955	92.6	68.1	24.5
January 1956	89.0	66.7	22.3
April 1956	(¹)	(¹)	(¹)
3-month average	91.8	68.0	23.8

[1] Not available.

TABLE 9.—*Chicken parts, frozen: Average selling price, purchase cost, and margin, by type of handler, July and October 1955, January and April 1956, and 4-month averages*—Continued

WINGS

Outlet, month, and year	Average selling price per pound	Average purchase cost per pound	Average margin per pound
Wholesalers:	*Cents*	*Cents*	*Cents*
Chicago:			
July 1955	34.9	31.9	3.0
October 1955	36.8	33.2	3.6
January 1956	35.5	30.6	4.9
April 1956	33.8	29.2	4.6
4-month average	35.2	31.2	4.0
Minneapolis-St. Paul:			
July 1955	33.3	30.2	3.1
October 1955	32.8	29.8	3.0
January 1956	30.2	28.2	2.0
April 1956	30.2	27.4	2.8
4-month average	31.6	28.9	2.7
Independent retailers:			
Chicago:			
July 1955	50.6	37.9	12.7
October 1955	46.5	34.6	11.9
January 1956	46.2	37.4	8.8
April 1956	45.5	33.7	11.8
4-month average	47.2	35.9	11.3
Minneapolis-St. Paul:			
July 1955	46.4	36.3	10.1
October 1955	48.6	38.8	9.8
January 1956	(¹)	(¹)	(¹)
April 1956	43.6	32.4	11.2
3-month average	46.2	35.8	10.4
Chain retailers:			
Chicago:			
July 1955	45.4	32.0	13.4
October 1955	46.5	29.2	17.3
January 1956	45.9	27.7	18.2
April 1956	42.9	28.1	14.8
4-month average	45.2	29.3	15.9
Minneapolis-St. Paul:			
July 1955	45.9	32.3	13.6
October 1955	44.3	33.6	10.7
January 1956	40.3	30.3	10.0
April 1956	37.0	27.0	10.0
4-month average	41.9	30.8	11.1

¹ Not available.

TABLE 9.—*Chicken parts, frozen: Average selling price, purchase cost, and margin, by type of handler, July and October 1955, January and April 1956, and 4-month averages*—Continued

LIVERS

Outlet, month, and year	Average selling price per pound	Average purchase cost per pound	Average margin per pound
Wholesalers:			
Chicago:	*Cents*	*Cents*	*Cents*
July 1955	120.0	100.0	20.0
October 1955	120.0	100.0	20.0
January 1956	120.0	100.0	20.0
April 1956	120.0	100.0	20.0
4-month average	120.0	100.0	20.0
Minneapolis-St. Paul:			
July 1955	142.0	126.8	15.2
October 1955	139.0	128.8	10.2
January 1956	126.0	105.8	20.2
April 1956	100.0	79.2	20.8
4-month average	126.8	110.2	16.6
Chain retailers:			
Chicago:			
July 1955	118.0	93.0	25.0
October 1955	118.3	95.2	23.1
January 1956	118.3	95.4	22.9
April 1956	118.1	92.4	25.7
4-month average	118.2	94.0	24.2
Minneapolis-St. Paul:			
July 1955	(¹)	(¹)	(¹)
October 1955	(¹)	(¹)	(¹)
January 1956	118.0	90.0	28.0
April 1956	(¹)	(¹)	(¹)
4-month average	(¹)	(¹)	(¹)

HEARTS

Wholesalers:			
Minneapolis-St. Paul:			
July 1955	22.9	21.5	1.4
October 1955	22.9	21.5	1.4
January 1956	(¹)	(¹)	(¹)
April 1956	27.0	24.0	3.0
3-month average	24.3	22.3	1.9

¹ Not available.

TABLE 9.—*Chicken parts, frozen: Average selling price, purchase cost, and margin, by type of handler, July and October 1955, January and April 1956, and 4-month averages*—Continued

GIZZARDS

Outlet, month, and year	Average selling price per pound	Average purchase cost per pound	Average margin per pound
Wholesalers:			
Chicago:	*Cents*	*Cents*	*Cents*
July 1955	(1)	(1)	(1)
October 1955	35.5	31.3	4.2
January 1956	34.0	31.0	3.0
April 1956	33.3	31.0	2.3
3-month average	34.3	31.1	3.2
Minneapolis-St. Paul:			
July 1955	33.1	30.4	2.7
October 1955	33.4	29.9	3.5
January 1956	30.2	28.2	2.0
April 1956	32.8	30.2	2.6
4-month average	32.4	29.7	2.7
Chain retailers:			
Chicago:			
July 1955	35.0	25.0	10.0
October 1955	38.2	26.7	11.5
January 1956	38.2	26.4	11.8
April 1956	36.8	25.4	11.4
4-month average	37.1	25.9	11.2
Minneapolis-St. Paul:			
July 1955	39.0	31.0	8.0
October 1955	(1)	(1)	(1)
January 1956	38.0	24.0	14.0
April 1956	39.0	28.0	11.0
3-month average	38.7	27.7	11.0

[1] Not available.

TABLE 10.—*Fowl, fresh (eviscerated): Average selling price, purchase cost, and margin, by type of handler, July and October 1955, January and April 1956, and 4-month averages*

Outlet, month, and year	Average selling price per pound	Average purchase cost per pound	Average margin per pound
Nearby processors:			
Chicago:	*Cents*	*Cents*	*Cents*
July 1955	38.7	31.4	7.3
October 1955	35.7	28.7	7.0
January 1956	38.4	31.6	6.8
April 1956	38.4	31.3	7.1
4-month average	37.8	30.8	7.0
Minneapolis-St. Paul:			
July 1955	37.3	28.2	9.1
October 1955	35.4	26.7	8.7
January 1956	35.7	28.7	7.0
April 1956	36.5	27.3	9.2
4-month average	36.2	27.7	8.5
Wholesalers:			
Chicago:			
July 1955	39.9	37.7	2.2
October 1955	37.5	32.9	4.6
January 1956	40.0	35.2	4.8
April 1956	39.2	36.0	3.2
4-month average	39.2	35.5	3.7
Minneapolis-St. Paul:			
July 1955	43.2	38.9	4.3
October 1955	40.8	38.3	2.5
January 1956	42.1	37.6	4.5
April 1956	45.0	41.5	3.5
4-month average	42.8	39.1	3.7
Independent retailers:			
Chicago:			
July 1955	50.8	41.0	9.8
October 1955	52.6	41.6	11.0
January 1956	46.9	37.6	9.3
April 1956	48.5	39.6	8.9
4-month average	49.7	40.0	9.7
Minneapolis-St. Paul:			
July 1955	48.8	39.3	9.5
October 1955	46.8	37.2	9.6
January 1956	46.4	38.0	8.4
April 1956	51.0	42.5	8.5
4-month average	48.3	39.3	9.0

TABLE 10.—*Fowl, fresh (eviserated): Average selling price, purchase cost and margin, by type of handler, July and October 1955, January and April 1956, and 4-month averages*—Continued

Outlet, month, and year	Average selling price per pound	Average purchase cost per pound	Average margin per pound
Chain retailers:			
Chicago:	*Cents*	*Cents*	*Cents*
July 1955	48.3	37.6	10.7
October 1955	48.1	37.8	10.3
January 1956	48.9	39.4	9.5
April 1956	48.5	37.9	10.6
4-month average	48.5	38.2	10.3
Minneapolis-St. Paul:			
July 1955	49.7	38.5	11.2
October 1955	53.2	37.2	16.0
January 1956	53.3	38.8	14.5
April 1956	55.9	40.4	15.5
4-month average	53.0	38.7	14.3

TABLE 11.—*Fowl, New York dressed: Average selling price, purchase cost, and margin, by type of handler, July and October 1955, January and April 1956, and 4-month averages*

Outlet, month, and year	Average selling price per pound	Average purchase cost per pound	Average margin per pound
Nearby processors:			
Minneapolis-St. Paul:	*Cents*	*Cents*	*Cents*
July 1955	27.8	20.8	7.0
October 1955	30.2	19.8	10.4
January 1956	32.0	22.7	9.3
April 1956	33.4	22.3	11.1
4-month average	30.9	21.4	9.5
Wholesalers:			
Minneapolis-St. Paul:			
July 1955	38.1	27.6	10.5
October 1955	36.6	29.8	6.8
January 1956	38.5	30.7	7.8
April 1956	35.6	25.9	9.7
4-month average	37.2	28.5	8.7

TABLE 12.—*Roasters, fresh: Average selling price, purchase cost, and margin, by type of handler, July and October 1955, January and April 1956, and 4-month averages.*

Outlet, month, and year	Average selling price per pound	Average purchase cost per pound	Average margin per pound
Independent retailers:			
Chicago:	Cents	Cents	Cents
July 1955	(¹)	(¹)	(¹)
October 1955	61.7	48.2	13.5
January 1956	58.3	46.7	11.6
April 1956	61.2	49.2	12.0
3-month average	60.4	48.0	12.4
Minneapolis-St. Paul:			
July 1955	(¹)	(¹)	(¹)
October 1955	58.9	46.8	12.1
January 1956	57.8	45.0	12.8
April 1956	52.5	41.3	11.2
3-month average	56.4	44.4	12.0
Chain retailers:			
Minneapolis-St. Paul:			
July 1955	64.9	47.5	17.4
October 1955	60.2	39.6	20.6
January 1956	59.0	40.0	19.0
April 1956	59.0	38.0	21.0
4-month average	60.8	41.3	19.5

¹ Not available.

TABLE 13.—*Capons and caponettes, fresh: Average selling price, purchase cost, and margin, Chicago independent retailers, July and October 1955, January and April 1956, and 4-month averages*

Outlet, month, and year	Average selling price per pound	Average purchase cost per pound	Average margin per pound
	Cents	Cents	Cents
July 1955	65.9	53.5	12.4
October 1955	68.7	56.6	12.1
January 1956	66.2	53.6	12.6
April 1956	63.1	50.4	12.7
4-month average	66.0	53.5	12.5

TABLE 14.—*Fowl, frozen (eviscerated): Average selling price, purchase cost, and margin, by type of handler, July and October 1955, January and April 1956, and 4-month averages*

Outlet, month, and year	Average selling price per pound	Average purchase cost per pound	Average margin per pound
Georgia, Alabama, and Arkansas processors:			
Chicago:	Cents	Cents	Cents
July 1955	43.7	30.7	13.0
October 1955	42.3	30.3	12.0
January 1956	41.7	29.7	12.0
April 1956	47.4	32.9	14.5
4-month average	43.8	30.9	12.9
Chain retailers:			
Chicago:			
July 1955	50.7	40.6	10.1
October 1955	49.6	39.0	10.6
January 1956	49.9	40.9	9.0
April 1956	49.4	38.7	10.7
4-month average	49.9	39.8	10.1

TABLE 15.—*Broilers: Number and value sold in 20 leading counties, 1954*

State and county	Broilers sold	Value
	Number	Dollars
Delaware–Sussex	57,716,993	38,361,499
Arkansas–Washington	17,190,821	9,858,468
Arkansas–Benton	16,894,517	10,400,461
Maryland–Wicomico	14,887,544	9,631,464
Mississippi–Scott	12,915,636	7,656,699
Georgia–Cherokee	12,723,945	7,482,325
Georgia–Hall	12,644,702	7,676,314
Maryland–Worcester	11,470,942	7,292,174
Georgia–Forsyth	11,125,356	7,655,249
Virginia–Rockingham	10,959,546	7,535,666
Texas–Gonzales	8,810,911	5,867,924
Texas–Shelby	8,217,863	5,467,409
Maine–Waldo	8,186,347	7,586,656
California–Los Angeles	7,697,177	7,177,438
Georgia–Whitfield	7,136,721	3,901,082
Maryland–Somerset	6,988,860	4,528,408
Pennsylvania–Lancaster	6,352,427	5,353,443
Maryland–Caroline	6,236,152	4,295,824
Georgia–Lumpkin	6,177,550	4,115,951
Connecticut–Windham	6,006,473	5,409,747

1954 Census of Agriculture, vol. 1, County Table 7 (pt. 2 of 2).

TABLE 16.—*Poultry: Number of broilers sold from certain States, 1954, and amount of processed poultry received at various markets, by State of origin, 1955*

State	Number of broilers sold [1]	Amount of processed poultry received [2]											
		New York	Chicago	Philadelphia	Detroit	Boston	Los Angeles	San Francisco	St. Louis	Cleveland	Cincinnati	Pittsburgh	Atlanta
	1,000	*1,000 pounds*	*1,000 pounds*	*1,000 pounds*	*1,000 pounds*	*1,000 pounds*	*1,000 pounds*	*1,000 pounds*	*1,000 pounds*	*1,000 pounds*	*1,000 pounds*	*1,000 pounds*	*1,000 pounds*
Georgia	114,369	9,666	35,739	272	27,935	---	3,252	221	2,855	11,673	4,149	1,852	2,817
Arkansas	62,337	508	8,381	---	182	2,931	8,651	4,845	8,953	18	---	---	---
Delaware	61,591	44,292	439	17,853	---	24	---	68	79	---	---	222	---
Texas	55,711	84	302	34	---	---	5,093	322	640	---	---	---	62
Maryland	46,094	63,319	658	16,014	1,774	4,695	571	42	---	1,592	238	883	161
Alabama	39,562	---	9,622	---	7,001	667	4,427	---	3,491	60	---	---	---
California	38,276	3,427	387	---	---	162	2,122	18,852	403	39	4,019	2,399	---
Virginia	37,044	7,193	135	2,879	372	478	---	---	---	40	1,268	525	16
North Carolina	35,464	12,277	423	457	1,322	---	---	---	---	42	---	---	---
Mississippi	34,390	---	163	---	75	---	2,228	---	2,941	---	---	---	---
Indiana	28,651	1,137	11,746	32	1,714	81	---	---	35	261	1,376	199	---
Pennsylvania	25,817	10,964	1,342	4,314	80	2,108	---	---	---	3,902	93	6,875	---
Maine	24,276	64,644	47	---	---	19,437	---	---	---	---	---	---	---
Missouri	20,065	1,799	1,809	236	78	105	101	249	4,208	166	67	188	---
West Virginia	18,991	581	31	5	82	---	---	---	---	---	27	1,858	---
Connecticut	15,667	25,948	69	70	---	808	---	---	---	---	---	---	---

[1] 1954 Census of Agriculture.
[2] Receipts of processed poultry at various cities, Dairy and Poultry Market News, AMS.

TABLE 17.—*Civilian per capita consumption: Broilers, farm chickens, and all chickens, ready-to-cook basis, 1940–56*

Year	Broilers	Farm chickens	All chickens [1]
	Pounds	*Pounds*	*Pounds*
1940	1.9	12.2	14.1
1941	2.7	12.7	15.4
1942	3.2	14.5	17.7
1943	4.2	18.8	23.0
1944	3.9	16.5	20.4
1945	5.0	16.6	21.6
1946	4.1	15.3	19.4
1947	4.3	13.8	18.1
1948	5.5	12.8	18.3
1949	7.1	12.5	19.6
1950	8.6	12.0	20.6
1951	10.4	11.3	21.7
1952	11.7	10.4	22.1
1953	12.3	9.6	21.9
1954	13.7	9.1	22.8
1955	13.7	7.7	21.4
1956	16.7	7.6	24.3

[1] Revised in 1957 on basis of unadjusted population.

Based on data from the Poultry and Egg Situation, Agr. Mktg. Serv. The 1957 Outlook Issue of the Poultry and Egg Situation, PES–186, shows the percentage of chicken meat that comes from specialized broilers, in table 20; table 9 of the May 1957 issue, PES–189, gives the revised data on consumption of all chickens.

CPSIA information can be obtained
at www.ICGtesting.com
Printed in the USA
LVHW081454211118
597922LV00011B/861/P